Christina. J. Clark

SECURE BUSINESS WEALTH

Mastering Lifetime Income

BY

CHRISTINA. J. CLARK

Christina. J. Clark

All right reserved. Do not publish any part of this publication in any form or by any means, including scanning, photocopying or otherwise without prior written permission to the copyright holder.

Copyright© 2024 By Christina. J. Clark

Christina. J. Clark

Christina. J. Clark

Table of Contents

INTRODUCTION

WHY SECURING BUSINESS WEALTH

ISIMPORTANT

CHAPTER 1

UNDERSTANDING WEALTH

CHAPTER 2

BUILDING A SOLID FINANCIAL

FOUNDATION

CHAPTER 3

BUSINESS WEALTH CREATION

Christina. J. Clark

CHAPTER 4

TAX PLANNING AND WEALTH

PRESERVATION

CHAPTER 5 WEALTH PLANNING

AND TRANSFER

CHAPTER 6

RETIREMENT AND SECURE WEALTH

CHAPTER 7

NAVIGATING ECONOMIC

CHALLENGES

MASTERING A FINANCIAL MINDSET

CASE STUDIES

Christina. J. Clark

INTRODUCTION

In an era of transforming financial landscapes and economic uncertainty, ensuring financial security and long-term prosperity has never been more important.

In this book "Secure Business Wealth: Mastering Lifetime Income," I explored the principles, strategies and actionable advice necessary to guarantee the financial well-being of your business and become skilled at generating a lifelong income.

This book is your complete guide, a roadmap designed to navigate the often-complex terrain of wealth creation, income generation, and financial security.

I recognize that the pursuit of long-term financial security requires a multi-pronged approach, combining proven methods and innovative thinking.

The carefully designed chapters in "Secure

Wealth in Business: Mastering Lifetime Income" are dedicated to a fundamental aspect of financial empowerment. From understanding the psychology of wealth, to building a solid financial foundation, discovering sources of income, and exploring the intricacies of tax planning and wealth preservation, it covers it all. The chapters will not only provide you with the knowledge to make informed financial decisions, but will also inspire you to take action, implementing the lessons learned to build a prosperous and more secure future.

With an emphasis on practicality and applicability, this book is not just a theoretical exploration but also a financial empowerment guide, providing you with a clear path to financial mastery. Along the way, I'll discuss essential concepts like tax-advantaged investing, creating multiple income streams, and the complexities of estate planning and asset transfers.

These concepts will guide you in developing a financial strategy that aligns with your goals and values. My goal is to give you the tools to achieve and maintain financial security, allowing you to live the life you want and ensuring your wealth lasts for future generations.

When you delve into the pages of "Secure Business Wealth: Mastering Lifetime Income," you begin a transformative journey toward financial independence and control of your financial future.

I sincerely hope that you will find the knowledge and advice in these chapters enlightening and thought-provoking, and that they will fully equip you to achieve your financial aspirations.

Now, embark on this enlightening journey to secure your business wealth and master the art of generating lifelong income

WHY SECURING BUSINESS WEALTH IS IMPORTANT

Financial security is the foundation of a fulfilling life. It allows you to pursue your passions, support loved ones, and make meaningful choices without worrying about financial instability. "Secure Business Wealth" recognizes the profound importance of ensuring your financial well-being. It's not just about accumulating wealth, it's also about the peace of mind that comes with knowing you have a solid financial plan.

In today's rapidly changing economic landscape, traditional notions of job security have become less reliable. Business owners face an ever-changing business environment, while employees face fluctuations in the job market.
In this context, having a comprehensive understanding of how to secure and grow your wealth is not just a luxury but a necessity. This journey is not a destination but an ongoing process: a lifelong commitment to financial prosperity.

Throughout this book, you will discover the fundamentals of wealth creation, income generation, and wealth preservation. You will learn how to build a solid financial foundation, whether you're an entrepreneur looking to expand your business's financial horizons or an individual seeking financial independence. The following pages will provide actionable strategies, practical examples, and expert advice to help you on your path to financial mastery. As you delve deeper into the chapters, you will gain the knowledge and confidence to overcome economic challenges, make informed investment decisions, and ultimately secure your financial legacy.

"Secure Business Wealth: Mastering Lifetime Income" is more than just a book; It's the roadmap for your financial future.
By embarking on this journey, you are taking the first step towards financial empowerment and ensuring you have the tools and knowledge you need to achieve a secure and prosperous life.

Christina. J. Clark

CHAPTER 1

UNDERSTANDING WEALTH

Defining Wealth and Financial Security

To pursue financial happiness, it is essential to start with a clear understanding of two basic concepts: wealth and financial security. People often use these terms interchangeably, but they represent distinct aspects of our financial lives. In this chapter, we will delve deeper into the definitions of wealth and financial security, providing a comprehensive understanding of these concepts and their importance in our lives.

Defining wealth

At its core, wealth is a multifaceted concept that includes more than just monetary assets. While wealth certainly includes financial resources, it includes more than just dollars and cents. Wealth is the abundance of valuable resources that an individual or organization possesses.

These resources can come in many forms:

- **Financial wealth:** This is a phrase that refers to the amount of money and assets a person or entity possesses, which can support their lifestyle, invest in new ventures, or achieve other financial goals. This includes cash, investments, real estate, and other assets that can be easily converted into money. It is a measure of your liquidity and currency value.

- **Material wealth:** This includes tangible assets such as real estate, personal property, and assets such as vehicles, jewelry, and works of art.

- **Human capital:** refers to the skills, knowledge, and experience possessed by an individual that can create economic value. Your skills, knowledge, education, and expertise contribute to your wealth. Human capital represents your potential to earn income over your lifetime.

- **Social capital:** refers to the value that is derived from social networks and connections. It encompasses the shared norms, values, trust, and reciprocity among members of a community or society, which facilitate cooperation and

  coordination. Social capital can be a valuable resource for individuals, businesses, and communities in achieving their goals and aspirations. Relationships and connections can be invaluable assets.
  Your network can open doors to opportunities, support, and collaboration that contribute to your overall wealth.

- **Intangible wealth:** refers to non-physical assets such as intellectual property, brands, patents, copyrights, and goodwill that contribute to the value of a company or an individual's net worth.

- **Well-being and health:** refers to a state of being healthy and feeling good, both physically and mentally. Good health and overall well-being are invaluable forms of wealth. Without health, all other forms of wealth may lose significance.

- **Time:** Time is a finite resource and can be considered as wealth. How you spend your time, especially in pursuing your goals and passions, contributes to your overall wealth.

Financial Security

Financial security is closely intertwined with wealth but represents a specific state within the broader landscape of wealth. It can be defined as the peace of mind that comes from having enough means to cover your basic needs and essential expenses without constant worry and financial stress.

Financial security includes several key elements:

- **Emergency fund:** Having an emergency fund with easily accessible savings to cover unexpected expenses is an important part of financial security. It provides a safety net when life's unexpected challenges arise.

- **Debt Management:** Managing and minimizing debt are essential to ensuring financial security. High-interest debt can harm your finances and hinder your ability to save and invest.

- **Income Stability:** A reliable source of income is vital for financial security. It ensures you can cover your regular expenses and work toward your financial goals.

- **Insurance Coverage:** Adequate insurance, including health, life, disability, and property insurance, protects you and your family from financial devastation in the face of unexpected events.

- **Savings and Investments:** Building savings and investments over time provides a cushion and an opportunity for wealth accumulation. Investments can generate income, which contributes to your financial security.

- **Retirement planning:** Preparing for retirement is an important aspect of financial security.

The Psychology of Wealth

The Psychology of Wealth is not merely a result of financial decisions and actions; it is deeply interconnected with the psychology of individuals. Understanding the psychology of wealth is essential to achieving and maintaining financial success. This involves recognizing the mental and emotional factors that influence financial behavior and decision-making.

This comprehensive exploration explores different aspects of the psychology of wealth:

- **Mindset and beliefs (Scarcity or abundance mindset):** A scarcity mindset stems from a fear of not having enough and viewing resources as limited. This mindset can lead to financial decisions motivated by fear, such as hoarding money, avoiding investments, or being too frugal. In contrast, the abundance mentality believes in the endless possibilities of wealth and prosperity in life. This encourages calculated risk-taking, investment, and seizing growth opportunities.

- **Limiting beliefs:** Many people have limiting beliefs about money, often shaped by childhood experiences and social conditioning. These beliefs can be self-sabotaging. For example, the belief that "money is the root of all evil" can lead to unconscious resistance to the accumulation of wealth. Identifying and challenging these beliefs can be liberating and enable individuals to pursue financial success without internal conflict.

- **Self-esteem and money:** Self-esteem and money are deeply connected. A person's self-esteem can have a significant impact on their financial behavior. People with low self-esteem may unconsciously engage in financially self-sabotaging behavior, feeling unworthy of wealth. Developing a strong sense of self-worth allows individuals to make decisions that are consistent with their financial goals.

- **Emotional factors:** Emotions play a central role in financial decisions. Fear can lead to impulsive decisions, such as selling off during a market downturn, while greed can lead to excessive risk-taking. Developing a resilience help

individuals make wise financial decisions and maintain a long-term perspective.

- **Delayed gratification:** The ability to delay gratification is an important psychological trait for wealth creation. This means choosing long-term financial goals over short-term pleasures. People who can delay gratification are more likely to save, invest, and build wealth over time.

- **Behavioral Economics (Loss Aversion):** The phenomenon of loss aversion is a powerful cognitive bias. People tend to fear loss more than they value equivalent gains. As a result, they often make overly conservative financial choices, such as avoiding investments or giving up profitable investments too early. Understanding this bias is essential to making sound investment decisions.

- **Confirmation bias:** Confirmation bias is the human tendency to seek information that confirms pre-existing beliefs while ignoring contradictory evidence. This can have a significant impact on financial decisions, as individuals may selectively seek out information that supports their views, leading to suboptimal choices. To overcome this bias, effective wealth builders actively seek out diverse perspectives and stay open to different perspectives.

- **Anchor:** Anchor is the reliance on the first information encountered when making a decision. This can affect financial negotiations and investment choices. Wealth creators should be aware of the effects of anchoring and strive to make objective, research-based decisions, rather than letting initial information unduly influence their choices.

- **Set and visualize goals:** Setting clear, specific, and motivating financial goals is critical to wealth creation. Goals provide direction and motivation, helping individuals stay on track on their financial journey.

- **Visualization:** Visualization is a powerful technique for solidifying financial goals. This involves imagining future financial success and can increase motivation and resilience in the face of challenges. Visualization helps individuals

- connect more deeply with their goals, making them more likely to persevere in their pursuit of wealth.

- **Financial identity:** People often have a financial identity, which is the ability to manage their money effectively. This identity corresponds to their beliefs about their financial capabilities. Recognizing and reshaping your financial identity can lead to healthier financial behaviors. For example, seeing yourself as a "frugal" person can inspire more responsible financial choices.

- **Cultural and social influences:** Social influences can have a significant impact on financial choices. Peer pressure, especially in consumer-driven societies, can lead to overspending and lifestyle inflation. Choosing friends and a community that supports your financial goals is important. Surrounding yourself with people who value financial responsibility can help you stay focused and disciplined.

- **Cultural Beliefs:** Cultural norms and values can shape attitudes toward wealth and financial decisions. Some cultures emphasize frugality, frugality, and community support, while others prioritize conspicuous consumption and personal achievement. Being aware of the influence of culture on financial choices can help individuals make informed decisions consistent with their values.

- **Risk Tolerance:** Understanding your risk tolerance is essential to successful investing. Some people are risk averse and prefer conservative, low-risk investments, while others are more risk-tolerant and open to higher-return, high-risk investments.

- **Emotional Intelligence:** Emotional intelligence, which includes recognizing and managing one's own emotions, plays a key role in making better financial decisions. It also helps to understand other people's emotions during financial negotiations. Being aware of your emotions can lead to more effective communication and negotiation skills, which is especially important in asset management and investing.

- **Behaviour change:** Effective wealth builders often use behaviour change strategies to align their financial behaviour with their goals. These strategies may include setting up automatic savings and investment contributions, creating financial habits, and using positive reinforcement to establish and strengthen good financial habits.

Income Streams in Secure Business Wealth

Income streams play a pivotal role in securing business wealth by providing stability, resilience, and opportunities for growth. Diversifying income sources is a fundamental strategy for businesses to mitigate risks associated with economic fluctuations, market volatility, and unexpected events. Let's delve into different types of income streams:

- **Primary income stream (Employment income):** Your primary source of income, usually from work, serves as the foundation for your financial life. It covers essential expenses, provides a sense of financial security and provides a basis for saving and investing.

- **Secondary Income Streams (Passive Income):** Passive income sources, such as investments and rental properties can gradually become more important and even replace primary income stream.

Examples include: dividends from stocks, interest from bonds, rental income from real estate, and royalties from creative work.

To maximize passive income, consider diversifying your investments and building a diversified portfolio. Diversification can help spread risk and ensure steady returns.

- **Business Income:** If you own a business, the income generated from it can be significant. To maximize your business revenue, prioritize growth, efficiency, and scalability. Explore ways

to grow your business, improve processes, and adapt to changing market conditions.
Diversify your products or services to capture additional revenue streams.

- **Side Jobs and Self-Employment:** Earning extra income through side jobs or self-employment can be a way to accelerate savings and investments. To maximize these income streams, consider learning additional skills or certifications that can increase your earning potential in your free time. In addition, make use of online platforms and networks to discover freelance opportunities.

CHAPTER 2

BUILDING A SOLID FINANCIAL FOUNDATION

Setting Financial Goals

Setting financial goals is an important step toward achieving financial success and building a secure future. Financial goals provide direction, motivation and a roadmap to manage your income, spending, savings and investments. This comprehensive exploration digs deeper into the importance of setting financial goals and offers ideas on how to do it effectively.

The importance of financial goals

- **Clarity and purpose:** Setting financial goals brings clarity and purpose to your financial life. Whether you want to buy a house, pay off debt, save for your children's education or retire comfortably, setting goals will help you stay focused and motivated.

- **Measurement and Accountability:** Financial goals are quantifiable, which means you can measure your progress. This metric allows you to hold yourself accountable for your financial decisions and track your journey to achieving your goals.

- **Prioritize:** Goals help you prioritize your financial efforts. When you have multiple goals, like saving for an emergency fund, paying off high-interest debt, and investing for retirement, setting goals allows you to allocate your resources accordingly.

- **Financial Security:** Objectives play an important role in enhancing financial security. For example, setting a goal to build an emergency fund will help you prepare for unexpected expenses, while setting a retirement savings goal will pave the way for a secure retirement.

Types of financial goals

- **Short-term goals:** These goals typically have a time frame of one year or less. Examples include paying off credit card debt, saving for a vacation, or building an emergency fund. Short-term goals act as stepping stones to long-term goals.

- **Mid-term goals:** Mid-term goals have a time frame of one to five years. Examples include saving for a down payment on a home, funding a college education, or buying a new car. These goals often require planning and consistent saving.

- **Long-term goals:** Long-term goals have a time frame of 5 years or more. These are often big, life-changing goals like planning for retirement, getting out of debt, or achieving financial independence. These goals require consistent, long-term commitment and planning.

Creating SMART Goals

Creating SMART goals is a proven method for setting objectives that are specific, measurable, achievable, relevant, and time-bound. Whether in personal development, business planning, or project management, employing SMART criteria helps individuals and teams focus their efforts effectively and track progress efficiently. Let's break down each component of SMART goals:

- **Specific:** Goals should be clear and unambiguous, answering the questions of what, why, and how. Specific goals provide a clear direction, avoiding confusion and ambiguity. Instead of setting a vague goal like "improve sales," a specific goal would be "increase monthly sales revenue by 20%."

- **Measurable:** Goals should be quantifiable, allowing for objective assessment of progress. Measurable goals provide tangible evidence of success and enable tracking of achievements. For instance, if the goal is to "improve customer satisfaction," a measurable goal would be "increase customer satisfaction ratings from 75% to 90% within six months."

- **Achievable:** Goals should be realistic and attainable within the resources and constraints available. Setting achievable goals prevents frustration and discouragement, maintaining motivation throughout the journey. It's crucial to assess the feasibility of goals based on available resources, skills, and time. For example, if a team aims to "double productivity in one month," it might not be achievable or realistic given the current capacity and resources.

- **Relevant:** Goals should align with broader objectives and be meaningful to the individual or organization. Relevant goals contribute directly to overall success and are essential in guiding actions and decisions. It's important to ensure that goals are relevant to the current priorities and strategic direction. For instance, if a company's priority is to expand its market share, setting a goal to "launch a new product line targeting a niche market segment" would be relevant.

- **Time-bound:** Goals should have a defined timeframe for completion, providing a sense of urgency and accountability. Time-bound goals prevent procrastination and ensure timely progress. Setting deadlines helps to prioritize tasks and allocate resources efficiently. For example, instead of saying "improve employee training," a time-bound goal would be "implement a new employee training program by the end of the quarter."

Now, let's walk through the process of creating SMART goals:

- **Identify the Objective:** Clearly define what you want to achieve. Whether it's personal development, business growth, or project completion, articulate the desired outcome.

- **Make it Specific:** Define the goal in precise terms. What exactly do you want to accomplish? Be clear and concise in describing the desired result.

- **Ensure Measurability:** Determine how you will measure progress and success. What metrics or indicators will you use to track your performance? Establish measurable targets or milestones.

- **Assess Achievability:** Evaluate whether the goal is realistic and attainable given your resources, skills, and constraints. Consider potential obstacles and determine if you have the capacity to overcome them.

- **Check for Relevance:** Confirm that the goal aligns with your broader objectives and priorities. Is it meaningful and significant in the context of your overall vision or strategy?

- **Set a Timeframe:** Establish a deadline or timeframe for achieving the goal. When do you intend to accomplish it? Define specific dates or timeframes to create a sense of urgency and accountability.

- **Review and Refine:** Periodically review your goals to track progress and make adjustments as needed. Assess whether you're on track to achieve your objectives, and modify your approach if necessary.

Creating a Budget and Financial Plan

Budgeting and financial planning are fundamental steps to achieving financial success, creating wealth, and securing your financial future. In this comprehensive guide, we'll explore the importance of budgeting and financial planning, and provide insight on how to create an effective financial plan and budget.

Importance of budgeting and financial planning

- **Financial awareness:** Financial planning and budgeting provide a clear picture of your financial situation. They help you understand where your money comes from and where it goes. This awareness is necessary to make informed financial decisions.

- **Control and Discipline:** Budgeting gives you control over your finances. It serves as a roadmap for your money, allowing you to allocate resources based on your priorities and financial goals. It also instils discipline in your spending habits.

- **Goal Achievement:** Financial planning and budgeting enable individuals to allocate resources towards accomplishing specific financial objectives. Either it's saving for a home, paying off debt or planning for retirement, a well-structured financial plan will ensure you're on track to achieve your goals.

- **Emergency Preparedness:** Budgeting includes setting aside funds for emergencies, providing a financial safety net when unexpected costs or crises arise. An emergency fund is an integral part of your financial plan.

How to Create a Budget

- **Gather financial information:** Start by gathering all of your financial information, including sources of income, bank statements, bills and receipts. Having a complete picture of your finances is essential.

- **Categorize income and expenses:** Categorize your income into different sources, such as salary, bonuses, investments, and rental income. As for expenses, categorize them into fixed costs (e.g. Mortgage, rent, utilities) and variable costs (e.g. groceries, entertainment).

- **Set financial goals:** Identify your financial goals and prioritize them. Your goals can range from short-term goals like paying off credit card debt to long-term goals like planning for retirement.

- **Income minus expenses:** Subtract your total expenses from your total income. This will give you first-hand insight into your financial situation, whether you spend more or less than you earn.

- **Create a spreadsheet or budgeting app:** Many people use spreadsheets or budgeting apps to manage their finances. These tools help you track your income, expenses, and savings over time.

- **Allocate funds:** Allocate your income to cover your expenses and achieve your goals. Make sure to set aside a portion of your income for savings and emergency funds. Be realistic about your spending and try to cut back on discretionary spending to make room for savings.

- **Review and adjust:** Review your budget regularly to make sure you're on track. Life changes, such as raises, additional expenses, or unexpected events, may require adjustments to your budget.

- **Evaluate your current financial situation:** Evaluate your assets, liabilities, and current net worth. This assessment provides the basis for your financial planning.

- **Emergency Fund:** Part of your financial plan should include establishing an emergency fund. Aim for at least three to six months' worth of living expenses saved in an easily accessible account.

Successful budgeting and financial planning strategies

- **Automatic savings:** Set up automatic transfers to your savings and investment accounts. Automating your savings ensures that you systematically allocate money to your goals.

- **Emergency Fund First:** Prioritize building your emergency fund before focusing on other financial goals. It provides a financial safety net in case of unexpected expenses or emergencies.

- **Debt reduction strategies:** If you have significant debt, consider aggressive debt reduction strategies. This may involve paying off high-interest debt first, negotiating lower interest rates with creditors, or consolidating loans.

- **Investing for the future:** In your financial plan, set aside a portion of your income for long-term investments. Diversify your portfolio to manage risk and potentially earn higher returns over time.

- **Reassess regularly:** Your financial plan is not set in stone. Evaluate your progress regularly and adjust your plan to reflect changes in your life, financial situation, and economic conditions.

.

- **Seek Financial advisor:** If you have complex financial goals or investments, consider consulting a financial advisor. They can provide you with expert knowledge and advice to help you make informed decisions.

Benefits of Budgeting and Financial Planning

- **Financial Security:** A well-structured financial plan and budget provides financial security by ensuring that You are prepared for emergencies and have a clear path to achieving your goals.

- **Debt reduction:** Budgeting and financial planning help you pay down debt more effectively, freeing up money for saving and investing.

- **Build Wealth:** A financial plan supports wealth creation by guiding your savings and investment strategies, helping you accumulate assets over time.

- **Retirement planning:** Financial planning includes retirement planning, ensuring that you are on track to retire comfortably and enjoy your golden years.

- **Peace of mind:** Financial planning and budgeting help reduce financial stress and provide peace of mind, knowing that you have a clear strategy for your financial future.

Budgeting and financial planning are essential steps on your path to financial success. It provides clarity, control and discipline in managing your money, helping you achieve your financial goals and providing a roadmap to secure your financial future. By integrating budgeting and financial planning into your financial habits, you can take control of your finances, reduce debt, build wealth, and ensure a prosperous and secure financial future.

Christina. J. Clark

Managing Debt

Debt management is an essential aspect of personal finance. Effective debt management can lead to financial freedom, reduced stress, and the ability to achieve your financial goals. here, we will explore the importance of debt management, strategies for reducing and eliminating debt, and the steps to take to get out of debt.

- **Debt Management Strategy (Debt Snowball Vs. Debt Avalanche):** These are two popular strategies for fighting lots of debt. In the debt snowball method, you prioritize paying off your smallest debt while making a minimum payment on the

  others. Once you've paid off your smallest debt, you move on to the next debt, and so on. This approach can give you a psychological boost by quickly eliminating small debts, which can motivate you to keep going.

In contrast, the debt avalanche method prioritizes debt with the highest interest rate. This method minimizes the total interest paid and can be more profitable in the long run. Choosing between these two strategies depends on your financial goals and psychological preferences.

- **Debt Consolidation:** Debt consolidation involves combining multiple high-interest debts into one lower-interest debt. This can simplify your monthly payments and potentially reduce the total interest you pay. Popular debt consolidation methods include personal loans, balance transfer credit cards, and home equity loans. However, it is essential to carefully evaluate the terms and fees associated with consolidation options to ensure they truly benefit your financial situation.

- **Negotiate with creditors:** You can often negotiate with creditors to reduce interest rates, reduce fees, or modify payment plans. This is especially true if you are experiencing financial difficulties. Creditors may be willing to work with you to ensure that you can make payments and avoid default.

- **Financial windfall:** If you receive a financial windfall, such as a tax refund, work bonus, or inheritance, consider putting some of it toward paying off debt. Agreements can significantly speed up your debt repayment and help you reach your goals faster.

- **Long-Term Debt Management Considerations:** Maintain Your Credit Score: As you work to reduce your debt, make sure to maintain your credit score. A good credit score is essential to getting favourable interest rates on loans, including mortgages. Continue paying your remaining debt on time, keep your credit card balances low, and avoid applying for new credit unless necessary.

- **Emergency fund:** Even as you focus on paying off debt, continue contributing and maintaining your emergency fund. This fund acts as a financial safety net, preventing you from accumulating new debt in the event of unexpected expenses or emergencies.

- **Lifestyle adjustments:** Consider making lifestyle adjustments to free up more money to pay off debt. This may include cutting back on discretionary spending, downsizing your living arrangements, or finding ways to increase your income through part-time work or self-employment opportunities.

- **Find professional help:** Reputable credit counselling agencies can provide valuable assistance to those struggling with debt. They offer budgeting advice, debt management plans, and debt education. Be sure to choose a nonprofit agency accredited by the National Foundation for Credit Counselling (NFCC).

- **Debt Management Plan:** Credit counselling agencies can also help you create a debt management plan (DMP) if you have multiple creditors. A DMP consolidates your unsecured debts into one monthly payment that the credit counselling agency distributes to your creditors. DMPs often come with reduced interest rates and fees.

- **Debt Resolution Program:** The debt resolution program involves negotiating with creditors to settle debts for less than the total outstanding balance. While this may reduce your total debt, it can negatively impact your credit score and lead to tax consequences for debt forgiveness. It is essential to carefully weigh the pros and cons of debt settlement.

Benefits of effective debt management

- **Financial freedom:** Managing and eliminating debt leads to financial freedom. When you pay off your debt, you'll have more income to save, invest, and reach your financial goals.

- **Improve credit:** Good debt management can improve your credit score, making it easier and more affordable to borrow money for big purchases like a house or car.

- **Reduce stress:** Debt can be a significant source of stress. By reducing and eliminating debt, you will feel less financial stress and more peace of mind.

- **Enhanced Financial Stability:** Effective debt management contributes to financial stability, allowing you to plan for your future and work toward long-term financial goals, such as retirement, homeownership, and wealth building.

Sustaining a Debt-Free Lifestyle

- **Budgeting and saving:** Once you've become debt-free, maintain a budget that prioritizes savings and investments. This ensures you continue to build wealth and remain financially secure.

- **Emergency Fund:** Continue to maintain your emergency fund. Your financial safety net is just as important when your debt-free, as it helps you handle unexpected expenses without resorting to credit.

- **Investing for the Future:** As your free up funds from debt repayment, consider redirecting those funds into investments, such as retirement accounts, stocks, or real estate, to build wealth over the long term.

- **Credit Responsibility:** After becoming debt-free, it's essential to continue using credit responsibly. Pay credit card balances in full each month, avoid carrying high balances, and be cautious about taking on new debt unless it aligns with your financial goals.

CHAPTER 3

BUSINESS WEALTH CREATION

Entrepreneurship and wealth

Entrepreneurship plays a central role in wealth creation and financial prosperity.

Entrepreneurs are individuals who identify opportunities, take calculated risks, and create value through their business activities.

In this chapter, we will explore the relationship between entrepreneurship and wealth, the steps to becoming a successful entrepreneur, and how entrepreneurship contributes to your wealth.

The relationship between entrepreneurship and wealth:

- **Scalability:** One of the main benefits of entrepreneurship is the scalability of business ventures. Successful entrepreneurs can expand their businesses to reach larger markets and generate higher profits. For example, technology startups can scale rapidly, potentially leading to significant financial success.

- **Multiple Streams of Income:** Entrepreneurship allows for multiple streams of income. Entrepreneurs can diversify their income streams by running multiple businesses, investing in different industries, or creating passive income streams.

- **Wealth Transfer:** Successful entrepreneurs can create wealth that can be passed on to future generations. Careful planning can ensure that the wealth created through business activities not only benefits the entrepreneur but also their heirs.

- **Exit Strategies:** Entrepreneurs often have the opportunity to achieve significant wealth through exit strategies such as selling their business or going public through an initial stock offering public offering (IPO).

Risks and challenges of starting a business

- **Financial risks:** Starting a business often involves potential financial risks, especially in the start-up phase. Entrepreneurs

- may invest their savings, apply for loans, or receive funding from investors, thereby risking their capital.

- **Time Commitment:** Running a business, especially in the early stages, can be time-consuming. Entrepreneurs often work long hours and make personal sacrifices to ensure their ventures succeed.

- **Market Competition:** Entrepreneurship is highly competitive, with many businesses vying for the same market share. Entrepreneurs must continually innovate and differentiate their offerings to stay ahead.

- **Regulatory Challenges:** Depending on the industry, entrepreneurs may face regulatory hurdles and compliance requirements that can be complex and time-consuming.

- **Asset Management for Entrepreneurs (Diversification):** Entrepreneurs who accumulate assets should diversify their investments to minimize risk.

Diversification can include investing in stocks, bonds, real estate, and other asset classes. It is also important to diversify your business interests to avoid being overly dependent on any one company.

Steps to Becoming a Successful Entrepreneur

- **Identify Opportunities:** Successful entrepreneurship begins with identifying opportunities in the market. This may involve recognizing unmet needs, gaps in existing products or services, or emerging trends.

- **Market Research:** Conduct thorough market research to validate your business idea. Understand your target audience, competitors, and the demand for your product or service.

- **Business Planning:** Develop a comprehensive business plan that outlines your business concept, target market, marketing strategy, financial projections, and a plan for scaling your business.

- **Funding:** Determine how you will finance your business. Options include self-funding, seeking investors, securing loans, or crowdfunding.

- **Execution:** Launch and manage your business effectively. This includes operations, marketing, customer service, and financial management.

- **Adaptability:** Be prepared to adapt to changing market conditions and consumer preferences. Successful entrepreneurs are flexible and open to pivoting their business strategies as needed.

- **Continuous Learning:** Entrepreneurship is a journey of continuous learning. Stay informed about industry trends, seek mentors or advisors, and invest in your own skills and knowledge.

The role of entrepreneurship in Wealth development

- **Income Generation:** Entrepreneurship provides an avenue for generating income that is not limited by traditional salary structures. Successful entrepreneurs have the potential to earn substantial profits.

- **Asset Accumulation:** Over time, profitable businesses can accumulate assets such as real estate, investments, and intellectual property, contributing to personal wealth.

- **Wealth Diversification:** Entrepreneurship allows individuals to diversify their sources of wealth. By building multiple successful ventures or investing in various business sectors, entrepreneurs can spread financial risk.

- **Job Creation:** As entrepreneurs grow their businesses, they often hire employees, contributing to job creation and helping others build their own financial security.

- **Innovation and Economic Growth:** Entrepreneurial ventures drive innovation, which can lead to economic growth and development. New businesses stimulate economic activity and generate tax revenue.

Types of Entrepreneurships

- **Small Business Entrepreneurship:** Many entrepreneurs start small businesses, such as restaurants, retail stores, and service providers. These ventures often serve local or niche markets.

- **Social Entrepreneurship:** Social entrepreneurs create businesses with the goal of solving societal or environmental issues.

These businesses focus on both profit and positive impact.

- **Tech Entrepreneurship:** Tech entrepreneurs build businesses in the technology sector, developing software, hardware, and digital platforms. These ventures often have high growth potential.

- **Franchise Entrepreneurship:** Franchise entrepreneurs operate businesses under established brands and business models. Franchise owners benefit from brand recognition and support.

- **Serial Entrepreneurship:** Serial entrepreneurs start and operate multiple businesses over their careers. They may sell businesses they've built and move on to new ventures.

Asset Maintenance and Management:

- **Investment Strategy:** Entrepreneurs who amass significant wealth often transition from active business ownership to investing in a variety of other assets each other, including stocks, bonds, real estate, and venture capital. An effective investment strategy is essential to maintain and grow wealth.

- **Wealth Preservation:** Wealth preservation strategies include risk management, estate planning, and tax optimization. These strategies help ensure that the wealth accumulated will last and continue to benefit the entrepreneur and their heirs.

- **Lifestyle and retirement planning:** Entrepreneurs should plan for their long-term financial well-being, including retirement. Retirement planning can involve creating retirement accounts, pension plans, and other financial tools to secure their future.

- **Balancing philanthropy:** Many entrepreneurs engage in philanthropy. Effective philanthropic planning can help entrepreneurs create meaningful impact while aligning with their values and goals.

Entrepreneurial Spirit and Skills

- **Innovation:** Entrepreneurs possess an innovative mindset and are willing to challenge the status quo. They are constantly

- looking for solutions to problems and looking for new opportunities.

- **Risk-taking ability:** Successful entrepreneurs are willing to take calculated risks. They understand that entrepreneurship inherently involves uncertainty and the possibility of failure.

- **Adaptability:** The ability to adapt to changing market conditions and consumer preferences is critical to business success. Entrepreneurs must be flexible and willing to adjust their business strategies when necessary.

- **Resilience:** Entrepreneurship often involves failures and challenges Resilience and the ability to learn from failures are essential qualities of entrepreneurs.

- **Entrepreneurship and social impact:** Some entrepreneurs focus on creating businesses with a strong social or environmental mission. Social entrepreneurs seek to solve pressing social problems while generating revenue.

- **Corporate Social Responsibility (CSR):** Established businesses, including those founded by entrepreneurs, often engage in corporate social responsibility initiatives. These initiatives involve philanthropy, sustainability efforts, and ethical business practices. Community Involvement: Entrepreneurs often play an active role in their local communities, supporting economic development, education, and charitable causes.

Strategies for growing a profitable business

Growing a profitable business requires a combination of effective strategies, careful planning, and continuous adaptation to market conditions and field changes. In these pages, we will Discover key strategies that can help you grow your business, increase profits, and achieve long-term success.

- **Market research and customer insights:** Market segmentation: Identify and segment your target market based on demographic, psychographic, and behavioural data. This allows you to tailor your products, services, and marketing efforts to specific customer groups.

- **Customer surveys:** Collect regular customer feedback through surveys and interviews

- **New product development:** Innovate by introducing new products or services that meet emerging customer needs or market trends. Be ready to change and adapt your offerings based on customer feedback.

- **Quality assurance:** Ensure the consistent quality of your products or services. High-quality services lead to customer loyalty and positive word-of-mouth marketing.

- **Marketing (Digital marketing):** Use online channels such as social media, content marketing, email marketing, and search engine optimization to reach a wider audience and engage with potential customers.

- **Content Strategy:** Create valuable and informative content that positions your business as an industry authority. This not only attracts potential customers but also builds trust and credibility.

- **Branding:** Invest in brand recognition and consistency. Your brand must communicate your values, mission, and unique selling points, helping customers identify your business.

- **Customer relationship management:** Customer Service Excellence: Provide exceptional customer service to build strong customer relationships and loyalty. Respond promptly to inquiries, resolve problems, and put customer satisfaction first.

- **Loyalty Programs:** Implement loyalty and rewards programs to encourage customer loyalty. Offer discounts, exclusive access, or points-based rewards to retain customers.

- **Personalization:** Personalize the customer experience by using customer data and insights to tailor offers, promotions, and communications.

- **Scalability and operational efficiency:** Continuously evaluate and improve your business operations. Streamline processes to reduce costs, improve productivity, and minimize waste.

- **Technology integration:** Invest in technology solutions that automate tasks and provide real-time data analytics. This can improve decision-making and efficiency.

- **Scalable Infrastructure:** Ensure your business infrastructure can handle growth. This includes software, hardware, and scalable physical locations where applicable.

- **Financial management:** Monitor and control operating costs, and look for opportunities to cut unnecessary costs. Cost control has a direct impact on profits.

- **Pricing Strategy:** Regularly review and adjust your pricing strategy based on market conditions, competition, and the value you provide to customers.

- **Cash flow management:** Maintain healthy cash flow by tracking income and expenses, managing accounts receivable, and having financial reserves for unexpected expenses.

- **Geographic expansion:** Consider expanding into new markets or geographies, either through physical locations or online sales.

- **Product Diversification:** Introduce complementary products or services that cater to your existing customer base or target a new market segment.

- **Strategic Partnerships:** Collaborate with other businesses to leverage their expertise, customer base, or distribution channels for mutual benefit.

- **Talent Management:** Attract and hire the right talent with the skills and expertise needed to support your business goals.

- **Training and Development:** Invest in ongoing training and development programs to ensure that your team is equipped to meet the challenges of growth.

- **Employee engagement:** Foster a positive work environment, encourage employee engagement, and recognize and reward outstanding performance.

- **Data-Driven Decision Making:** Use data analytics and key performance indicators (KPIs) to measure the effectiveness of your strategies. Tailor your approach based on data-driven insights.

- **Market Trends:** Stay informed about industry trends and emerging technologies. Adjust your strategy to accommodate these developments.

- **Feedback loops:** Establish customer, employee, and stakeholder feedback loops to gather valuable information for decision-making.

- **Risk management:** Identify potential risks and develop contingency plans to minimize their impact. Be prepared to face unexpected challenges or disruptions.

- **Market Research:** Stay informed about market conditions, economic trends, and geopolitical factors that may impact your business.

- **Legal and regulatory compliance:** Ensure your business complies with applicable laws and regulations to avoid legal and financial consequences.

- **Monitoring and Measurement:** Regularly evaluate your business performance applying key metrics. This includes financial metrics (profit margins, revenue growth) and operational metrics (customer retention, employee productivity). Regularly assess internal operations to identify areas that can be improved and ensure compliance with best practices.

- **SWOT Analysis:** Perform a SWOT (strengths, weaknesses, opportunities, threats) analysis to evaluate your company's current position and plans for the future.

- **Strategic planning:** Build a long-term vision and a clear strategic plan for your business. Describe goals, milestones, and the steps needed to achieve them.

- **Agile approach:** Be flexible and adapt to changing market conditions. Your strategic plan must allow for adjustments based on changing circumstances.

- **Online Presence and E-Commerce:** If possible, consider expanding your business to the online market. E-commerce can open up new revenue streams and allow you to reach a broader customer base.

- **Mobile Optimization:** Make sure your website and online presence are mobile-friendly. With the increasing usage of

- smartphones for online shopping, mobile optimization is crucial for accessibility and customer experience.

- **Digital marketing expertise:** Invest in digital marketing strategies, such as pay-per-click advertising, social media advertising, and search engine optimization (SEO), to increase your online visibility and reach potential customers.

- **Integrate feedback:** Act on customer feedback by improving and adapting your products, services, and customer interactions.

Transparently communicate how feedback affects your business decisions.

- **Supply Chain Optimization:** Supplier Relations: Strengthen supplier relationships to achieve favorable terms, reliable delivery, and savings. Collaborative partnerships can create mutual benefits.

The Importance of Diversification:

Diversification is a fundamental concept in both investment and business strategies. It involves spreading risk and resources across a range of different assets or activities to achieve a more balanced and stable portfolio or business model. Diversification is recognized as a critical strategy for managing risk, promoting sustainability, and increasing the potential for long-term success. In this section we will explore the significance of diversification in secure business wealth.

- **Risk Mitigation:** Diversification is primarily about risk management. It's the equivalent of not putting all your eggs in one basket. By spreading investments or business activities across different assets, industries, or markets, you reduce the risk of a substantial loss if one asset or market underperforms. This risk mitigation is essential in uncertain and volatile environments.

- **Volatility Reduction:** One of the immediate benefits of diversification is the reduction of overall portfolio or business volatility. Different assets or business segments may react differently to economic or market events. While one asset might be experiencing a downturn, another could be performing well. This helps to stabilize returns and prevent extreme fluctuations.

- **Asset Allocation and Optimization:** Diversification is closely tied to asset allocation strategies. For investors, this involves determining the right mix of asset classes (stocks, bonds, real estate, etc.) based on individual financial goals, time horizons, and risk tolerance. For businesses, it means optimizing resource allocation to different product lines, markets, or divisions. Efficient asset allocation allows for a balance between risk and return.

- **Long-Term Wealth Preservation:** Diversification is crucial for preserving wealth over the long term. In the context of investing, it helps protect the capital you've worked hard to accumulate. This is especially vital for retirement planning, where the focus is on preserving and growing wealth to sustain your lifestyle for years to come.

- **Enhanced Risk-Return Profile:** While diversification doesn't eliminate risk, it can enhance the risk-return profile of your portfolio or business. It allows for the combination of high-risk, high-reward investments or activities with lower-risk, more stable ones. This way, you can aim for competitive returns while managing risk effectively according to your financial objectives.

- **Adaptability and Resilience:** Diversification promotes adaptability and resilience. It equips investors and businesses to weather unexpected changes or downturns in a more agile way. Diversified portfolios and business structures are less susceptible to a single negative event having a catastrophic impact.

- **Market Opportunities and Growth:** In the context of businesses, diversification provides opportunities for market expansion and growth. By offering a variety of products, services, or entering new markets, businesses can tap into previously untapped customer segments. This growth potential can significantly increase revenue and profitability.

- **Innovation and Competitive Advantage:** Diversification can foster innovation and create a competitive edge. A business that consistently adapts to changing

    market demands by introducing new products or services can stay ahead of competitors and remain relevant in the marketplace. This innovation can be a powerful driver of growth.

- **Sustainability and Risk Management:** Business diversification is closely linked to sustainability. A diversified business structure is less susceptible to external shocks, such as economic downturns, market volatility, or changes in consumer preferences. This mitigates risk and contributes to long-term sustainability.

- **Capital Allocation:** Efficient capital allocation is another critical aspect of business diversification. Businesses need to

- allocate resources to different segments or divisions based on their performance and growth potential. By optimizing the allocation of financial and human resources, businesses can enhance profitability and resource efficiency.

- **Geographical Diversification:** For businesses operating in different regions or countries, geographical diversification can provide an extra layer of risk mitigation. It can reduce the impact of regional economic downturns, political instability, or natural disasters in a specific area. It also allows businesses to tap into diverse consumer markets and benefit from regional economic conditions.

- **Mergers and Acquisitions (M&A):** Mergers and acquisitions strategies are a form of business diversification. Through acquisitions or mergers, businesses can enter new markets, acquire new customers, and expand their product or service offerings. M&A can also led to operational efficiencies, cost savings, and synergies, enhancing the overall strength of the business.

- **Competitive Advantage and Market Relevance:** Diversification ensures that your business remains adaptable and relevant in a dynamic marketplace. By

offering a variety of products or services, you can attract a wider customer base and respond to changing consumer preferences and trends. This competitive advantage is essential for long-term success.

- **Sustainable Growth and Longevity:** Business diversification supports sustainable growth and longevity. It allows businesses to adapt to evolving market conditions, minimize risks, and expand their reach. By continually innovating and exploring new opportunities, diversified businesses are better positioned to thrive over the long term.

CHAPTER 4

TAX PLANNING AND WEALTH PRESERVATION

Understanding Taxation

Taxation is a fundamental aspect of modern society, playing a pivotal role in government funding, wealth redistribution, and economic regulation. In this section, we'll explore the various facets of taxation, including its purpose, types, principles, and strategies for managing and optimizing your tax liability.

Purpose of Taxation

- **Taxation serves multiple purposes:** Funding Government Operations: Taxes provide governments with revenue to finance public services and infrastructure, such as education, healthcare, defence, and law enforcement.

- **Wealth Redistribution:** Progressive tax systems aim to reduce income inequality by imposing higher tax rates on the wealthy and lower rates on lower-income individuals.

- **Economic Regulation:** Tax policies can influence economic behaviour. For example, tax incentives may encourage investment in specific sectors or industries.

- **Stabilizing the Economy:** In times of economic crisis, governments may adjust tax rates to stimulate or restrain economic activity.

Types of Taxes

Taxes can be categorized into several types:

- **Income Taxes:** Collected on individuals' and businesses' earnings, income taxes include federal, state, and local income taxes.

- **Sales Taxes:** Imposed on the sale of goods and services. These can be state or local sales taxes and may be subject to exemptions.

- **Property Taxes:** Levied on the value of real estate properties, such as homes or land. Property taxes fund local government services.

- **Corporate Taxes:** Applicable to business profits, corporate taxes vary by country and may be subject to deductions and credits.

- **Excise taxes:** They are often applied to specific products such as cigarettes, alcohol, or gasoline. Excise taxes are used to regulate consumption and fund government initiatives.

- **Capital gains tax:** Charges profits from the sale of assets, such as stocks or real estate.

Tax- Efficient Investing

Tax-efficient investing is a strategy to optimize your investment returns by minimizing risk. By carefully managing your investments, you can legally reduce your tax liability and keep more of your profits. In this section, I will explore the principles, strategies, and considerations of tax-efficient investing.

Key principles of tax-efficient investing

- **Asset location:** Placing assets in the appropriate type of account can have a critically important impact on tax efficiency. In general, it's best to keep tax-inefficient investments, such as bonds or actively traded assets, in tax-efficient accounts such as IRAs or 401(k)s. Tax-efficient investments, such as index funds or tax-managed funds, may be suitable for taxable brokerage accounts.

- **Tax-Delayed Growth:** Investments held in tax-efficient accounts, such as traditional IRAs and 401(k)s, can grow tax-deferred. This means you don't have to pay taxes on capital gains, dividends, or interest until you withdraw the money, which can allow your investments to compound more effectively.

Tax-Efficient Funds

Funds designed with tax efficiency in mind can minimize the impact of capital gains distributions and provide lower tax consequences. Index funds and ETFs (Exchange-Traded Funds) are often tax-efficient options.

- **Holding term:** Long-term investments (typically held for more than one year) are subject to lower long-term capital gains tax rates, making them more tax efficient.
- **Short-term investments**: may result in higher tax rates. Tax Loss Capture is a strategy that

involves selling investments at a loss to reduce your tax liability.

- **Dividend Yield:** Consider the tax implications of stocks or funds with high dividend yields. Paying high dividends can lead to higher taxable income.

Strategies for Tax-Efficient Investing

- **Asset Allocation:** Create a diversified portfolio that fits your financial goals while considering the tax efficiency of each investment. This involves balancing different asset classes to meet your risk tolerance and return goals.

- **Tax-efficient Funds:** Invest in funds designed to minimize capital gains distributions. Passively managed funds, such as index funds and ETFs, typically have lower turnover and may be more tax-efficient than actively managed funds.

- **Minimize turnover:** High portfolio turnover can lead to increased capital gains distributions. Minimize turnover by holding long-term investments and choosing funds with low turnover.

- **Municipal Bonds Consideration:** Municipal bonds typically provide tax-free interest income at the federal and in some cases state levels. They can be a tax-efficient way to generate income.

- **Tax-efficient Withdrawals:** When withdrawing money from your retirement accounts, plan strategically to minimize your tax liability. This may involve managing withdrawals to maintain a lower tax bracket or delaying Social Security benefits.

Considerations For Tax-Efficient Investing

- Consider investments with tax advantages, such as municipal bonds, which offer tax-free interest income, or index funds that offer lower revenue, reducing capital gains distributions.

- **Estate Planning:** Plan a strategic transfer of your assets to your heirs to minimize estate taxes. Techniques may include gifts, setting up a trust, or using the annual gift tax exemption.

- **Stay informed:** Stay up to date with tax law changes and changes. Being aware of adjustments to tax rates, deductions, and credits can help you make informed financial decisions.

- **Tax laws and regulations:** Stay up to date on changes in tax laws and regulations. Tax policies may change, which will affect your investment strategy. Be aware of any tax code changes that may affect your investments.

- **Investing assets:** Carefully consider which assets should be held in taxable accounts and which should be kept in tax-advantaged accounts. Optimize your property investments for tax efficiency.

- **Rebalancing:** Periodically rebalance your portfolio to maintain your target asset allocation. However, be aware of the tax consequences of selling and buying assets.

- **Professional advice:** Seek advice from financial professionals, such as a financial advisor or tax professional, who can help you implement a tax-efficient investment strategy that suits your needs.

CHAPTER 5

WEALTH PLANNING AND TRANSFER

The activities of wealth planning and transfer are vital for individuals and families to effectively manage and distribute their assets. These involve deciding what happens to someone's assets, properties, and wealth after they pass away or become unable to make decisions. Wealth planning that is effective can bring peace of mind, safeguard assets from excessive taxes, and guarantee a smooth wealth transfer to intended beneficiaries. Wealth planning provides asset protection by shielding against creditors, lawsuits, and financial liabilities.

Proper structuring can shield assets from risks, Minimizing Tax Liabilities well-thought-out wealth planning strategies can significantly reduce asset taxes, gift taxes, and income taxes, thus preserving more wealth for beneficiaries. Wealth planning allows individuals to specify how assets should be distributed, ensuring that they go to the right individuals and charitable organizations according to their wishes.

Key Components of Wealth Planning

- **Will:** A will is a legally binding document that outlines how an individual's assets should be distributed upon their death. It can also name guardians for minor children and specify the executor of the estate.

- **Trusts:** Trusts are versatile tools used to manage and distribute assets. They can help reduce asset taxes, protect assets, and provide for specific needs of beneficiaries.

- **Power of Attorney:** A power of attorney document authorizes someone to make financial or healthcare decisions on your behalf if you become unable to do so.

- **Healthcare Proxy and Living Will:** These documents designate a person to make healthcare decisions for you and outline your healthcare preferences in the event of incapacitation.

- **Beneficiary Designations:** Review and update beneficiary designations on life insurance policies, retirement accounts, and investment accounts to ensure assets go to the intended recipients.

Wealth Transfer Strategies

- **Gifting:** Making lifetime gifts to beneficiaries can reduce the size of the taxable assets and provide financial support during one's lifetime.

- **Irrevocable Life Insurance Trust (ILIT):** ILITs hold life insurance policies outside the estate to avoid estate taxes. The trust is the owner and beneficiary of the policy.

- **Family Limited Partnership (FLP) and Family Limited Liability Company** (LLC): These entities allow for the orderly transfer of assets to family members while maintaining control and reducing tax liability.

- **Charitable Giving:** Philanthropic giving can be integrated into the wealth plan to support charitable causes and reduce asset taxes.

- **Generation-Skipping Transfer (GST) Trusts:** These trusts enable wealth to be transferred to grandchildren or more remote generations while avoiding generation-skipping transfer tax.

Professional Involvement in Wealth Planning and Transfer

Wealth planning and transfer can be complex, and it is advisable to seek the expertise of professionals such as:

- **Estate Planning Attorney:** An attorney specializing in wealth planning can draft and review legal documents, ensuring they comply with state and federal laws.

- **Financial Planner:** Financial Planner can help individuals create a comprehensive financial plan that fits their estate planning goals and objectives.

- **CPA or Tax Advisor:** These professionals can provide advice on reducing tax liability in wealth planning, helping to optimize wealth transfer strategies.

- **Trustee or Executor:** The appointment of a trustee or executor can ensure that the wealth plan is carried out as planned.

Regularly reviewed and updated Estate plans should be periodically reviewed and updated to reflect changes in personal circumstances, tax laws and financial goals.

Life events such as marriage, divorce, and family births and deaths may require adjustments to the estate plan.

The importance of wealth planning and transfer

- **Asset protection:** Wealth planning plays an important role in protecting your assets from various threats, such as creditors, litigants or bankrupts. Depending on how your wealth plan is structured, certain assets may be protected against potential claims, providing a level of security for your beneficiaries.

- **Minimize tax liability:** Wealth planning is important to minimize tax liability that can erode the value of your assets. Key considerations include federal estate taxes, gift taxes, and intergenerational transfer taxes. Effective strategies, such as gifts, trusts and tax-efficient asset allocation, can help reduce this tax burden.

- **Control asset distribution:** Wealth planning allows you to decide how your assets will be distributed after your death. This is especially important if you have specific wishes about who will inherit your assets or if you want to make charitable contributions. Without a clear plan, state laws regarding intestate succession will determine the distribution of assets, which may not be in accordance with your wishes.

- **Avoid family conflict:** Incomplete or unclear estate planning can lead to conflict between family members, potentially leading to lengthy legal battles. Well-drafted documents and open communication with beneficiaries can help prevent conflicts and ensure a smoother transition of assets.

- **Incapacity planning:** wealth planning involves more than just distributing assets after death. It also involves preparing for incapacitation that may result from illness or injury. Documents such as durable powers of attorney and advanced health care directives designate trusted people to manage your financial and medical affairs when you cannot do so.

CHAPTER 6

RETIREMENT AND SECURE WEALTH

Preparing For Retirement

Preparing for retirement is a major financial and lifestyle transition that requires careful planning and consideration. In this section, I will walk you through the key steps and considerations to ensure a safe and enjoyable retirement.

- **Learn about retirement planning Assess your financial situation:** Start by assessing your current financial situation. This includes calculating your savings, investments, assets, and liabilities. Understanding where you stand financially is the first step in planning for retirement.

- **Determine Your Retirement Goals:** What does retirement look like to you? Consider factors such as where you want to live, the activities you want to pursue, and any special goals or dreams you have for your retirement years

- **Set a Retirement Age:** Decide when you plan to retire. This age can be flexible, but having a target retirement date helps in creating a retirement savings timeline.

- **Building Retirement Savings Start Saving Early:** The sooner you begin saving for retirement, the better. Compound interest can significantly boost your savings over time. Contribute regularly to retirement accounts like a 401(k) or an Individual Retirement Account (IRA).

- **Contribute to Employer Plans**: If your employer offers a retirement plan, such as a 401(k), take full advantage of it. Contribute at least enough to receive your employer's matching contribution because this is essentially free money.

- **Diversify your investments:** Diversification helps spread risk. Invest in a mix of assets, including stocks, bonds, and other investments, to earn better returns while managing risk.

- **Consider additional savings accounts:** Besides employer-sponsored plans, explore what other retirement savings options, such as IRAs offer tax advantages.

- **Calculate Retirement Expenses:** Determine your expected monthly and annual expenses in retirement. Consider costs like housing, healthcare, food, transportation, and entertainment.

- **Factor in Healthcare Costs:** Healthcare expenses tend to increase in retirement. Investigate Medicare and consider long-term care insurance to help mitigate potential healthcare costs.

- **Inflation:** Account for inflation when estimating your future expenses. What costs $1,000 today could cost a lot more in 10 or 20 years.

- **Budget for Your Retirement Lifestyle:** Craft a detailed budget that covers all your expected expenses. This will help ensure you have enough income to support your desired lifestyle in retirement.

- **Emergency Fund:** Maintain an emergency fund to cover unexpected expenses in retirement. This safety net can prevent you from dipping into your retirement savings prematurely.

- **Retirement Income Plan (Social Security):** Understand how Social Security benefits work and when you're eligible to receive them. Delaying a claim may result in higher monthly payments.

- **Pension plans:** If you have a pension, know the terms of your plan as it will provide you with a steady income in retirement.

- **Investment income:** Consider how you will generate income from your investments. You may need to tap into your retirement account to manage it in a tax-efficient manner.

- **Review and adjust your plan:** Update your retirement plan regularly. As you approach retirement, review your financial situation and adjust your plan as needed. Make sure your investments align with your risk tolerance and financial goals.

- **Budgeting after retirement:** Budget for your life after retirement, taking into account changes in your spending habits and any unexpected expenses.

- **Wealth planning:** Consider how you want to manage your assets in retirement and beyond. Write or update your will, designate beneficiaries, and make arrangements for any potential long-term care needs.

- **Seek Professional Advice Financial Advisor:** Consult with a certified financial advisor who can provide you with expert advice on retirement planning, investment strategies, and strategies Withdrawals are tax-advantaged.

- **Legal Advisor:** You may want to consult with a wealth planning attorney to ensure your assets are protected and distributed according to your wishes.

Retirement Income Strategies

- **Traditional Pension Plans:** Traditional pension plans, also known as defined benefit plans, offer a reliable source of retirement income. Employers contribute to these plans during an employee's working years, and the payout is typically based on a formula considering factors such as years of service and salary. This strategy provides financial security because retirees receive a predetermined monthly income, often indexed to inflation. However, they are becoming less common in the private sector, with many companies turning to defined contribution plans like 401(k)s.

- **Social Security**: Social Security is a government-guaranteed source of retirement income, funded by payroll taxes. Retirees are eligible to receive benefits at age 62, with full retirement age ranging from 65 to 67, depending on year of birth. Delaying benefits until age 70 can result in higher monthly payments. Deciding when to apply for Social Security is an important decision that must take into account factors such as life expectancy and other sources of income. 401(k) and IRAs: 401(k) plans and IRAs are tax-advantaged retirement savings accounts. They allow individuals to contribute pre-tax or post-tax money and invest it in a variety of assets. When retirees withdraw from these accounts, they may face taxation.

Managing these withdrawals strategically, such as taking advantage of lower tax brackets, is a key part of the strategy. Additionally, converting traditional IRAs to Roth IRAs can provide tax-free income in retirement.

- **Annuities:** Annuities are financial contracts offered by insurance companies. Annuities provide a guaranteed lifetime income stream in exchange for a one-time payment. Deferred annuities allow funds to accumulate before converting them into a source of income. While they offer stability, they come with fees and limited liquidity. It is essential to understand the terms before purchasing an annuity.

- **Systematic withdrawal plan:** Systematic withdrawal plan involves taking a fixed percentage of your portfolio each year. The 4% rule suggests withdrawing 4% of the initial value of the portfolio in the first year, taking into account inflation in subsequent years. However, market performance and asset allocation play an important role in the sustainability of this strategy. Retirees should be cautious and possibly adjust their withdrawals based on the performance of their portfolio.

- **Dividend-paying stocks and bonds:** Investing in dividend-paying stocks and bonds can provide a steady stream of income. Dividend stocks are shares of companies that distribute a portion of their profits to shareholders. Bonds pay interest regularly. While these investments provide income, they are subject to market fluctuations and may require active portfolio management to maintain desired income levels.

- **Real estate investments:** Real estate investments, such as rental properties, can generate rental income. This strategy combines asset price appreciation with continued cash flow. However, property management can be time-consuming and the real estate market can be volatile. Additionally, liquidity may be limited because selling one asset is not as simple as selling other assets.

- **Long-Term Care Insurance:** Long-term care insurance is an essential part of retirement planning. It covers the cost of expanded medical services that Medicare may not cover. Planning for potential health care costs is essential to avoid depleting retirement assets and ensuring a secure financial future.

- **Delay retirement:** Some people choose to delay retirement, which has several financial advantages. Staying in the workforce longer allows them to continue saving and investing, reducing their years to retirement, increasing Social Security benefits and giving retirement assets more time to grow.

Christina. J. Clark

CHAPTER 7

NAVIGATING ECONOMIC CHALLENGES

Economic Downturns and Financial Resilience

Economic downturns are periods of negative economic growth characterized by declining GDP, rising unemployment, falling consumer spending, and decreasing business investment. These downturns can occur due to various factors such as financial crises, recessions, or external shocks like natural disasters or pandemics. While economic downturns are a natural part of the economic cycle, they can have significant social and financial implications, often leading to hardships for individuals, businesses, and governments.

Financial resilience refers to the ability of individuals, businesses, and economies to withstand

and recover from economic downturns. It encompasses various factors including financial stability, risk management, adaptability, and resourcefulness. Building financial resilience is essential for mitigating the adverse effects of economic downturns and ensuring sustainable economic growth over the long term.

Causes of Economic Downturns

- **Financial Crises:** Financial crises often stem from excessive speculation, unsustainable debt levels, or failures in financial regulation. Examples include the subprime mortgage crisis of 2008 or the Asian financial crisis of 1997.

- **Recessions:** Recessions are typically caused by a combination of factors such as a decrease in consumer spending, tightening of credit conditions, or declines in business investment.

- **External Shocks:** Natural disasters, geopolitical conflicts, and pandemics like COVID-19 can trigger economic downturns by disrupting supply chains, reducing productivity, and increasing uncertainty.

Impact of Economic Downturns

- **Unemployment:** Economic downturns often lead to layoffs and job losses as businesses cut costs to survive. High unemployment rates can exacerbate poverty and social inequality.

- **Decreased Consumer Spending:** During downturns, consumers tend to cut back on discretionary spending, leading to decreased demand for goods and services, further dampening economic activity.

- **Business Failures:** Weak demand, reduced access to credit, and declining revenues can push businesses into bankruptcy, leading to layoffs and reduced investment.

- **Government Budget Deficits:** Lower tax revenues and increased spending on unemployment benefits and social welfare programs can result in government budget deficits during economic downturns.

Strategies For Surviving Economic Downturn

- **Build and Maintain an Emergency Fund:** An emergency fund is your financial safety net. Its role becomes especially crucial during economic crises. It ensures that you have cash reserves to cover unexpected expenses, like medical emergencies or job loss, without resorting to high-interest debt. The key is not just creating the fund but also maintaining it. Regular contributions and revisiting the fund's size as your life circumstances change are essential. Ideally, you should have enough money to cover at least 3 to 6 months of living expenses.
- **Create a budget and stick to it:** Your budget is your financial roadmap. It helps you track your income and expenses, allowing you to effectively manage your finances in times of crisis. Faced with economic challenges, the

budget serves as a priority tool. You can spend your limited resources on essential expenses like housing, utilities, groceries, and healthcare.

Additionally, it helps you identify discretionary expenses that can be temporarily reduced to save money.

- **Debt reduction:** High-interest debt, especially credit card balances, can worsen financial hardship during a crisis. Interest rates can rise quickly, making it difficult to regain financial stability. Prioritize paying off high-interest debt as quickly as possible. Consider consolidation or balance transfer options to reduce interest rates, allowing you to pay off your debt more efficiently.

- **Diversify Your Income:** Relying solely on a single source of income can be risky, especially during economic downturns when job security may be uncertain. Explore opportunities for additional income streams. This might include part-time work, freelancing, or monetizing skills and hobbies. Diversifying your income helps reduce financial vulnerability and enhances your overall financial stability.

- **Prioritize Essential Expenses:** When an economic crisis hits, it's important to differentiate between essential and non-essential expenses. Prioritize your spending over essentials like housing, utilities, groceries, and healthcare. Consider postponing or reducing non-essential expenses such as dining out entertainment, and non-urgent home renovations. By focusing on the essentials, you can maintain your cash flow to meet your important needs.

- **Preserving your retirement savings:** Your retirement savings are a long-term investment and withdrawing them early can have long-term consequences. Avoid using your retirement account during an economic crisis as this can result in penalties and tax liability. Instead, rely on your emergency fund and other sources of liquidity to meet your immediate financial needs. Keeping your retirement savings intact will ensure your long-term financial security.

- **Find Out About Government Assistance:** During severe economic crises, government assistance programs may be available to assist individuals and families in need. These programs may include unemployment benefits, food assistance, and housing assistance. If you qualify, apply for these programs to help close the financial gap during difficult times.

- **Review and adjust investment portfolio:** Economic crises can lead to significant declines in investment portfolios. The key strategy here is to avoid panic selling. Markets tend to recover over time, and selling investments during an economic downturn can result in irreparable losses. Instead, review your asset allocation and risk tolerance to ensure they align with your long-term financial goals.

Make thoughtful adjustments, when necessary, based on your financial plan, rather than reacting to short-term market fluctuations.

- **Consider workforce and cost reductions:** In situations where an economic crisis results in prolonged financial difficulties, consider making changes on a larger scale. This could include downsizing your home, selling unnecessary possessions, or moving to a more affordable area. By reducing your living costs, you can ease financial pressure and create a more sustainable budget that fits your current financial situation.

- **Health and Insurance:** Adequate health insurance is important in times of economic crisis. Medical costs can be a significant financial burden, and good insurance can provide financial protection. Review your insurance policy to make sure you have the right coverage for your needs.

  Be aware of deductibles, out-of-pocket costs, and any changes in your insurance situation due to job loss or changes in income.

- **Continuously update your skills:** Developing skills improves your employability and earnings. Investing in education and skills development during an economic crisis can help you secure better job opportunities and career advancement when conditions improve. Consider taking courses, certifications, or training programs that align with your career goals and adapt to the changing job market.

- **Maintain Financial Discipline:** Emotional decisions during times of crisis can lead to financial mistakes. To avoid impulsive actions, stick to your financial plan, based on your long-term goals. Staying disciplined and making decisions based on rational judgment rather than emotional reactions is important during times of economic turmoil.

- **Seek professional advice:** A financial advisor or planner can provide you with valuable information, strategies, and support tailored to your specific situation. Their expertise can help you more effectively navigate difficult economic conditions, make informed decisions, and maintain financial stability.

- **Long-term planning:** While addressing immediate financial challenges is necessary, maintaining a long-term vision is also important. Economic crises are often temporary in nature, and by sticking to your financial plan, you can position yourself for recovery and long-term financial success.

    By continuing to invest in your financial future, even during an economic downturn, you can take full advantage of growth opportunities as conditions improve.

- **Psychological resilience:** Mental and emotional resilience is an essential part of surviving an economic crisis. Seek support from friends and family and consider stress reduction methods, such as exercise, meditation, or therapy, to maintain your mental health. Maintaining a positive attitude and focusing on growth opportunities can help you persevere through difficult times.

Christina. J. Clark

Christina. J. Clark

CHAPTER 8

MASTERING A FINANCIAL MINDSET

Developing a **wealth mindset**

A wealth mindset, often called an abundance mindset, is a mental attitude and set of beliefs that align with the idea that there is unlimited opportunity for wealth and success. This involves adopting a positive and empowering perspective on money, finances, and life in general.

The wealth mentality is characterized by several key attributes:

- **Abundance beliefs:** People with a wealth mentality believe that there is more than enough to go around. They see opportunities everywhere and don't see success as a limited resource.

- **Positive self-talk:** A rich mindset includes constructive self-talk. People with this mindset avoid negative, self-limiting beliefs and instead use positive affirmations to increase their self-esteem and potential.

- **Overcoming Challenges:** Instead of fearing failure, individuals with a wealth mindset view challenges and failures as learning opportunities. They don't let failures discourage them but see them as stepping stones to greater success.

- **Goal-oriented:** A rich mindset is goal-oriented. This involves setting specific, measurable, achievable, relevant, and time-bound (SMART) financial goals and taking consistent steps to achieve them.

- **Gratitude and positivity:** People with an abundance mindset practice gratitude daily, focusing on what they have rather than what they lack. This positive attitude attracts more positive experiences.
- **Challenging Scarcity Beliefs:** Developing a wealth mindset often begins with challenging and reframing scarcity beliefs. Scarcity beliefs are thoughts and attitudes that limit one's potential and create a sense of limitation. These beliefs can include thoughts like "I'll never have enough money," "There's not enough to go around," or "Money is the root of all evil. To challenge scarcity beliefs, recognize the scarcity belief that may be holding you back. This self-awareness is a crucial first step.
- **Reframe Beliefs:** Replace these limiting beliefs with more empowering and positive

ones. For example, replace "I will never have enough money" with "I am constantly improving my financial situation."

- **Affirmations:** Use positive affirmations to reinforce these new beliefs. Affirming these beliefs over and over can help you rethink your thinking over time.

- **Goal setting and visualization:** A rich mindset involves setting clear financial goals and visualizing their achievements. When setting financial goals, consider the following:

Specificity: Goals should be specific and describe exactly what you want to achieve.

Measurability: Goals should be measurable so you can track your progress.

Achievability: Set goals that are realistic and achievable given your current circumstances. Avoid setting goals that are too far away.

Relevance: Make sure your goals align with your aspirations and financial values. They must align with your long-term vision.

Time limit: Set a deadline to achieve your goal. This creates a sense of urgency and responsibility.

- **Financial Education:** Reading and Research, continue reading books, articles, and resources on personal finance, investing, and creating wealth as an integral part of a thriving Heritage state of mind.

- **Courses and Workshops:** Sign up for finance courses or attend workshops that can provide structured training to increase your financial knowledge.

- **Professional advice:** Seeking advice from financial professionals, such as a financial planner or investment advisor, will help you make informed financial decisions and strategies.

- **Risk-taking:** A wealth mindset includes taking calculated risks. This means weighing the potential rewards against the potential losses before making a decision.

- **Financial discipline:** Creating and sticking to a budget helps you allocate your income effectively, save, and invest wisely. Set savings goals and consistently save a portion of your income. This builds a financial cushion for future opportunities and emergencies.

- **Investment Strategy:** Develop an investment strategy aligned with your financial goals and risk tolerance. A long-term perspective and a disciplined approach to investing are fundamental components of a wealth mindset.

- **Giving Back and Philanthropy:** A wealth mindset extends to giving back and philanthropy. Many people with this mindset thrive by contributing to causes they care about, sharing their wealth, and making a positive impact on the world.

Overcoming Financial Obstacles:

Overcoming financial obstacles is a critical aspect of achieving financial success and security. Life often presents various challenges that can hinder one's ability to manage money, save, invest, and build wealth. These obstacles can be both external and internal in nature.

This section explores the most common financial obstacles and strategies for overcoming them.

- **Debt Management:** Debt is one of the most common financial obstacles. High-interest credit card debt, student loans, mortgages, and personal loans can quickly accumulate and become burdensome.

Overcoming debt includes:

- **Create a repayment plan:** Create a systematic plan to pay off your debt, prioritizing high-interest debt first.

- **Budgeting:** Implement a budget to control spending and allocate more funds to debt repayment.

- **Debt Consolidation:** Discover how to consolidate high-interest debt into a low-interest loan.

- **Find additional sources of income:** Consider part-time work, freelance opportunities, or side hustles to supplement your main income.

- **Lack of financial literacy:** Lack of financial literacy can lead to poor financial decision-making. To overcome this obstacle, you need to strive to continually learn about personal finance, investing, and money management through books, courses, and seminars.

- **Professional Advice:** Contact your financial advisor or planner for insight and guidance.

- **Emergency Expenses:** Unexpected financial emergencies, like medical bills or car repairs, can disrupt your financial plans. To overcome this obstacle, establish an emergency fund to cover unexpected expenses and build a financial cushion so you don't have to rely on a loan.

- **Insufficient savings:** Insufficient savings can affect your long-term financial security. To overcome this obstacle, you should set up automatic transfers to your dedicated savings account.

- **Goals:** Set clear savings goals for specific purposes. For retirement, education, and buying a home.

- **Investment Challenges:** Investing wisely is crucial for wealth accumulation, but it can be challenging. Strategies for overcoming this obstacle include learning about different investment options, risk tolerance, and investment strategies.

- **Diversity:** Spread investments across various asset classes to reduce risk.

- **Financial Emergencies:** Unplanned financial emergencies such as medical expenses can affect financial stability. To addressing this challenge, ensure you have adequate insurance (health, home, auto) to mitigate potential financial shocks.

- **Unplanned Life Events:** Life events such as divorce, job loss, and death in the family can have a significant financial impact. Strategies to address these challenges include having an Emergency Fund to handle sudden changes in your life without relying on debt.

- **Lifestyle Inflation:** As incomes rise, people often spend more, leaving little room for savings and investment. To overcome this, maintain a budget to manage your spending and provide additional income for savings and investments.

- **Psychological Barriers:** Emotional and psychological factors can interfere with making sound financial decisions. To overcome this, Practice self-awareness and emotional control when making financial decisions.

- **Procrastination:** Procrastinating on financial decisions can hinder your progress. To overcome this, Set clear deadlines for your financial tasks. For example, creating a budget or reviewing investments.

- **Accountability:** Share your financial goals with trusted friends and family who will hold you accountable.

- **Retirement Planning:** Neglecting retirement planning can lead to insufficient savings later in life. To solve this problem, start saving for retirement as early as possible to benefit from overall growth.

CHAPTER 9
CASE STUDIES

Success stories of Individuals who achieved lifetime income Mastery:

Warren Buffett

Warren Buffett, often referred to as the "Oracle of Omaha," is renowned for his exceptional investment acumen. He started investing in stocks at a young age and learned the principles of value investing from his mentor, Benjamin Graham. Over time, he built Berkshire Hathaway into a conglomerate of diverse businesses, including insurance, energy, and consumer goods. Buffett's approach focuses on buying companies with a competitive advantage, holding them for the long term, and reaping the benefits of compounding returns. His disciplined strategy and unwavering commitment to his principles have made him one of the wealthiest people in the world.

Oprah Winfrey

Oprah Winfrey's journey to lifetime income mastery is a testament to the power of resilience and entrepreneurship. Raised in poverty, she overcame personal challenges to become a media icon. Her eponymous talk show, "The Oprah Winfrey Show," became a global phenomenon, making her a household name. Oprah diversified her income by creating her own media company, Harpo Productions, and later, the Oprah Winfrey Network (OWN). She also ventured into publishing with "O, The Oprah Magazine." Oprah's philanthropic efforts, such as her leadership academy for girls in South Africa, demonstrate how lifetime income mastery can be used to make a positive impact on society.

Christina. J. Clark

Elon Musk

Elon Musk's success story is marked by his visionary approach to technology and innovation. He co-founded Zip2, an online business directory, which he sold to Compaq for $307 million. Musk then invested in and co-founded companies like PayPal, Tesla, SpaceX, Neural ink, and The Boring Company. These ventures span industries from electric vehicles and space exploration to advanced neurotechnology. Musk's journey highlights the importance of staying true to one's vision, even in the face of adversity and leveraging innovation to create multiple income streams.

CONCLUSION

In conclusion, "Secure Business Wealth: Mastering Lifetime Income" offers a comprehensive guide to achieving lasting financial stability in the ever-evolving landscape of business and finance. Through meticulous exploration of strategies, principles, and actionable insights, this book equips readers with the tools necessary to safeguard and grow their wealth over time. By emphasizing the importance of long-term planning, risk management, and adaptive thinking, it empowers individuals to navigate the complexities of wealth accumulation with confidence and resilience.

Furthermore, "Secure Business Wealth: Mastering Lifetime Income" underscores the significance of adopting a holistic approach to wealth management, integrating both personal and professional spheres to create a robust foundation for enduring prosperity.

By delving into the intricacies of asset allocation, diversification, and income generation, it enables readers to cultivate a resilient financial ecosystem capable of withstanding economic fluctuations and unforeseen challenges. With each chapter, readers are guided towards a deeper understanding of the interconnected elements that contribute to sustained wealth creation and preservation. Ultimately, this book serves as not only a roadmap to financial success but also a testament to the power of knowledge, discipline, and strategic foresight in securing a prosperous future for generations to come.

As we embark on the journey towards financial security, may the principles outlined in this book serve as a beacon, illuminating the path to a prosperous and secure future.

Christina. J. Clark

www.ingramcontent.com/pod-product-compliance
Lightning Source LLC
Chambersburg PA
CBHW050300230526
45471CB00005B/1961